A RABBIT FOR KIM JONG-IL

KIT BROOKMAN

Currency Press, Sydney

GRIFFIN
THEATRE
COMPANY

CURRENT THEATRE SERIES

First published in 2015
by Currency Press Pty Ltd,
PO Box 2287, Strawberry Hills, NSW, 2012, Australia
enquiries@currency.com.au
www.currency.com.au

in association with Griffin Theatre Company

Cataloguing-in-publication data for this title is available from the National
Library of Australia website: www.nla.gov.au

Typeset by Dean Nottle for Currency Press.
Cover design by RE:.
Front cover shows Steve Rodgers.

Currency Press acknowledges the Traditional Owners of the Country on which
we live and work. We pay our respects to all Aboriginal and Torres Strait
Islander Elders, past and present.

Contents

A Rabbit for Kim Jong-il was first produced by Griffin Theatre Company at SBW Stables Theatre, Sydney, on 10 October 2015, with the following cast:

FELIX	Kit Brookman
SOFIE AMSEL	Kate Box
JOHANN WERTHEIM	Steve Rodgers
PARK CHUN-HEI	Mémé Thorne
CHUNG DAE-HYUN	Kaeng Chan

Director, Lee Lewis
Designer, Elizabeth Gadsby
Lighting Designer, Luiz Pampolha
Composer & Sound Designer, Steve Francis
Stage Manager, Charlotte Barrett

CHARACTERS

JOHANN WERTHEIM, a German rabbit breeder

CHUNG DAE-HYUN, a North Korean government official

SOFIE AMSEL, a pet store attendant

FELIX, an extraordinarily large rabbit

PARK CHUN-HEI, a North Korean government official

POSTAL EMPLOYEE (to be played by the actor playing Felix)

SETTING

Germany, Belarus and North Korea, 2006.

NOTES

Punctuation is sometimes used to indicate delivery and does not always conform to the rules of grammar.

This play went to press before the end of rehearsals and may differ from the play as performed.

SCENE ONE

Germany, 2006, a small town outside of Bonn. The house of Johann Wertheim. A nice house but not cared for, the house of a distracted man. CHUNG DAE-HYUN, *elegant, inscrutable, and utterly out of place, sits on an old, worn armchair. Where the house is a mess,* CHUNG *is impeccably turned-out, where the house speaks of chaos,* CHUNG'*s manner is one of hard-won and unflinching containment. He waits patiently. After a moment,* JOHANN WERTHEIM, *unkempt, unwashed, and on edge, enters.*

WERTHEIM: Are you sure you're comfortable?

> CHUNG *looks at him.*

I know there are no springs in that, it'll be collapsing beneath you. No-one has sat in that chair for a very long time. People don't normally come into the house they just come to the barn, take a look, and off they go again, most aren't interested in me. Not that I take your sitting there as a sign of having any particular interest in me, I mean I know why you're here, I'm not naïve. Been around. Seen my fair share of—probably not a patch on what you've had to—never mind. I couldn't find the cushion I mentioned, I'm sorry, but I did find this bottle of schnapps and I thought, with you being new to the country and not widely travelled, I mean do you have the opportunity to get schnapps where you're from? I tend to imagine things like this as being a rare commodity, highly controlled. I imagine that only the high-ups can get stuff like this. I shouldn't pry. But you can imagine, I mean I'm sure you can imagine that it would be fascinating, for me. You're not stupid. I can tell that. And you speak German very well.

CHUNG: Thank you.

WERTHEIM: I only mean there can't have been much opportunity to really practise your speaking, your accent in particular. Who would you speak to?

CHUNG: Hostages.

WERTHEIM: Yes, well.

CHUNG: Hostages live as long as anyone else if you look after them.

WERTHEIM: Makes sense. How silly of me! But the schnapps, that'll be a treat. I don't normally drink this time of day but this is a bit of an occasion, isn't it? You've come all this way. Cheers.

CHUNG: Cheers.

WERTHEIM: How do you like it?

CHUNG: Very much, thank you.

WERTHEIM: I'm glad, Mr Dae-hyun.

CHUNG: Mr Chung.

WERTHEIM: Oh, on your card—

CHUNG: Yes, I know. The family name comes first.

WERTHEIM: Right.

CHUNG: In Korea.

WERTHEIM: Right, my apologies.

CHUNG: To new friends.

WERTHEIM: To new friends, yes. Have you been to Germany before?

CHUNG: No. It's been enjoyable, using the language. You are right, there are not many German speakers where I'm from. The language is not viewed as a priority. I learnt with the assistance of a book and a collection of CDs. I was joking about the hostages.

WERTHEIM: Yes, oh yes, of course, *Ha ha!* that's exactly what I—

CHUNG: A piece of advice given to me before I left was that although I may speak the language proficiently I may not have the necessary nuance to indicate when I'm joking, so I was advised not to joke, but it doesn't sit well with my nature.

WERTHEIM: Well. If you can't laugh…

CHUNG: What?

WERTHEIM: Hm?

CHUNG: What happens if you can't laugh?

WERTHEIM: Oh, just, everyone needs to laugh. It's a human… you know. Make light of things. Break the tension.

He drops his glass of schnapps onto the carpet.

Sweaty palms. Don't worry, it'll just soak in.

CHUNG: You can clean it up if you—

WERTHEIM: No no, we have important things to discuss. It really will soak in. I know it looks like it's pooling but just ignore it, really, let me pull up a chair.

CHUNG: Are we doing business now?

WERTHEIM: Oh—yes, alright. Down to business. Of course, it's obvious why you're here, people only come here for one reason, and it's not to see me or to enjoy my schnapps, people only come for one reason, the reason you're here, they come for Felix.

CHUNG: For the rabbit.

WERTHEIM: For the rabbit. Exactly. Although interest has dropped off lately. There was a lot of interest early on, when the pictures got onto the internet. Mostly from local news stations, wanting to get a picture of the rabbits. No-one took it seriously, no-one was interested in my reasons for nurturing Felix, for creating him. I was just the last item on the news, a crackpot living alone outside of Bonn who liked rabbits.

So I was surprised to hear from you, but happy! This is a very time-consuming one-man operation, and so lately in order to take care of the rabbits I've had to cease going to my regular workplace and obvious consequences have followed regarding my employment. So it was a very opportune moment that you got in touch, because I wasn't really sure how much longer I could... hang on.

Maybe things on the internet take longer to reach you, I understand that there's something of a filter.

CHUNG *gives nothing away.*

Or maybe not, maybe not at all. And all this is not to say I'm desperate, that I'm just, ah, just make me an offer and there we are! Because this is just temporary, I have qualifications. I could get another job like that, just like that.

CHUNG: We don't doubt your professionalism, Mr Wertheim. Your results speak for themselves. We're sure that we can come to a mutually beneficial arrangement.

WERTHEIM: Yes, mutually beneficial, I mean that's what it's all about, helping out, absolutely, ah, comrade. So, another schnapps? I'll have another. Oh, there are hairs on the glass, let me—

CHUNG: Not for me, thank you. I don't wish to be rude but I don't normally drink at this time of day.

WERTHEIM: No no, me neither, but if you don't mind on this particular occasion I'll just—oops—never mind.

He's poured a full-to-the-brim glass. He licks his hand.

Do you mind if I check before we, just in case we are able to arrive at a mutually satisfactory beneficial arrangement, I mean how were you intending to pay?

CHUNG: Cash.

WERTHEIM: Great.

CHUNG: If we reach an arrangement the handover will take place at the conclusion of our meeting.

WERTHEIM: Today?

CHUNG: I will be leaving the country tonight.

WERTHEIM: Yes, I've just—I mean it's nothing, I'm just helping my mother move house this afternoon and she's quite old.

CHUNG: You can help your mother tomorrow.

WERTHEIM: We've just lined up the truck and—

CHUNG: I will be leaving the country tonight.

WERTHEIM: Yes, you did mention.

CHUNG: If this is to happen, Mr Wertheim, in a mutually beneficial manner, it will need to happen according to my timetable.

WERTHEIM: I see. Well. She has to love me, I'm her son after all.

CHUNG: Ah, the conditions of love.

WERTHEIM: What?

CHUNG: Never exactly free, is it?

> *Slight pause.*

WERTHEIM: I assume that you were happy with Felix when you saw him, in the barn.

CHUNG: The rabbits were slightly smaller than we had been led to believe. Thinner, in fact.

WERTHEIM: Food has been getting short, it's not a cheap operation, I'm… right at my limit.

CHUNG: Felix is the one in the pictures?

WERTHEIM: Yes. Felix is the largest, but there are a number of breeding pairs, eight breeding pairs.

CHUNG: We will take them all. Including Felix.

WERTHEIM: Oh, I hadn't thought… I can't part with all of them. It's been a very long time I've spent reaching this point. You saw Felix. My pride and joy. He weighs fifteen kilograms. The size of a small goat. It's taken many generations of breeding to arrive at Felix. If you take all my breeding pairs I'll have to—

CHUNG: We will need all the breeding pairs. We could simply begin breeding smaller rabbits, as you have done, and build our way up over the years, but we don't have the time.

WERTHEIM: I see. Obviously you will need me to visit, to consult, to help you set up the proper arrangements and—

CHUNG: No, that will not be necessary.

WERTHEIM: But then how will I see my rabbits?

CHUNG: Unfortunately the offer is not open to negotiation.

WERTHEIM: I understand. I do understand, Mr Chung. It's a generous offer and… I will just need to take a moment—

CHUNG: Of course.

WERTHEIM: They're my friends.

I've looked into their grey eyes every morning for the last three years, the eyes of their parents and grandparents for years before that. I've felt their fur grow coarse as they've aged, fed them from my hand and nurtured them all their lives. They are my company, Mr Chung. My first waking thought. Last thing I see before I sleep.

CHUNG: Mr Wertheim, please appreciate that I am an agent with particular instructions. I am not authorised to negotiate, simply to issue our offer. I can inform you that it is our only offer. Take some time to think it over, if you must. But not too long.

WERTHEIM: I understand there is a famine in your country.

> CHUNG *gives nothing away.*

I can't imagine what you were thinking when you stepped out of your car and looked at the place.

CHUNG: I was thinking how clean the air tasted. And how far I was from home.

WERTHEIM: They must trust you.

> CHUNG *gives nothing away.*

I mean—you hear—I mean, lots of defections.

CHUNG: People are free to come and go from the Democratic People's Republic. Here I am, after all.

WERTHEIM: Yes.

CHUNG: I think that—and excuse me if this is an issue with my understanding of German—but I think that 'defections' is quite a strong term.

WERTHEIM: Well, yes, maybe it is.

CHUNG: It's true that it is rare for someone to leave the DPRK, but why would we? We have everything we want. With some small, quite brilliant exceptions. Like your rabbits.

WERTHEIM*'s phone begins to ring (it eventually stops).*

Would you like to get that?

WERTHEIM: It'll only be my mother.

All of them. Of course it makes sense, but I never thought that someone would want all of them. I was beginning to doubt that anyone cared at all. I can't tell you, Mr Chung, how it feels to know that what I've done here will be appreciated, that it won't have been for nothing. I only wish that I could come with you, to help.

CHUNG: I'm afraid that's impossible.

WERTHEIM: Then I do have a request, a personal request, of you, Mr Chung.

CHUNG: I'm not sure that I can… alright.

WERTHEIM: If I could ask you to please keep me informed as to how the breeding program progresses, if it's a success. And an update on Felix and the others from time to time.

CHUNG: I can assure you they will be well looked-after, Mr Wertheim.

WERTHEIM: Oh yes, Mr Chung, I really don't doubt, but this is just a personal request. Between new friends. Just every so often, send me a photograph and a few words.

CHUNG: That assumes that my relationship with the rabbits will continue after they have been acquired. The acquisition of the rabbits was my entire brief, Mr Wertheim.

WERTHEIM: But you're not going to leave them with strangers?

CHUNG: Am I not a stranger?

WERTHEIM: Well, I've met you, Mr Chung, I know you. And I saw— earlier, in the hutch, I saw how you handled the rabbits. You're a trained veterinarian, aren't you?

CHUNG *gives nothing away.*

I knew as I watched you that I would be handing over my rabbits to a man who knew how to care for them.

CHUNG: There are many people in my country who possess the necessary skills, Mr Wertheim.

WERTHEIM: Yes, but you, Mr Chung, you care, which is different. I could see it. I know that you understand why I make this request of you. Just a photograph. Every so often.

CHUNG: Mr Wertheim, I can't guarantee that it will be possible to send you a photograph. [*Utterly sincere*] I very much admire what you've been able to accomplish, Mr Wertheim, the ambition of it. I've never seen anything like them.

WERTHEIM: Oh. Thank you.

CHUNG: I am also trying to—I also have…

Slight pause.

You should know, Mr Wertheim, that the interest in your rabbits has come from the highest place in my country.

WERTHEIM: Yes, I—oh.

CHUNG: They will be well-cared-for.

WERTHEIM: You mean—that he, that he has seen—that, uh, Mr Kim—

CHUNG: The Dear Leader was very impressed with your rabbits, Mr Wertheim. With Felix especially. Very impressed.

WERTHEIM: Oh. Did he… communicate this to you… personally?

CHUNG *gives nothing away.*

Oh, I won't pry. Forgive me, it's in my nature to ask questions. I'm unused to… censoring myself.

CHUNG: No-one is asking you to censor yourself, Mr Wertheim. Here are the documents that you will need to sign forbidding disclosure of our agreement to anyone else.

WERTHEIM: You know I… lived in Leipzig, before the wall—do you know about the wall? Yes. I was still a young man when it came down, but I have some appreciation of… I *understand*, Mr Chung.

CHUNG: Would you like to sign the papers now?

WERTHEIM: I'm trying to tell you that—

CHUNG: Mr Wertheim?

WERTHEIM: Yes, yes.

CHUNG *takes out some papers from his briefcase and rests them on the briefcase cover for* WERTHEIM *to sign.*

You mentioned from the highest places in your country, from—

CHUNG: From the Dear Leader.

WERTHEIM: From him, from… the Dear Leader, yes. How did he, I mean how did he come across—?

CHUNG: On the internet, Mr Wertheim.

WERTHEIM: Just browsing?

CHUNG: He was inspired by a dream to search you out, Mr Wertheim. He knew of you long before he searched for you through Google.

WERTHEIM *'s phone begins to ring again.*

Do you wish to answer?

WERTHEIM: Not particularly. I'll just—

He tugs the cord out from the wall. He goes to sign.

Am I breaking some sort of—this may seem—but are there sanctions against your country that I should be—?

CHUNG: Everything has been arranged, Mr Wertheim.

WERTHEIM: Well.

He signs.

There we are.

CHUNG: And this is for you.

He hands over the briefcase.

Count it if you wish.

WERTHEIM: Oh, I'm sure—

CHUNG: Count it, Mr Wertheim. We won't speak again, so this will be your only chance.

The sound of a car horn.

That will be Felix's transportation.

WERTHEIM: Oh, I… thought I might just have a moment. Just me and the rabbits, before they go. Just a moment—between us, Mr Chung, ah… bit afraid I might… I didn't want anyone else to be around when I said goodbye, I'm a bit afraid I might get a bit weepy.

CHUNG: Over a fucking rabbit?

Pause.

WERTHEIM: Excuse me?

CHUNG: [*suddenly with a heavy accent, but genuinely attempting to recover*] Oh, did I—my German was bad? Oh, so sorry.

WERTHEIM *reaches out a hand for the papers.* CHUNG *pulls them away.*

WERTHEIM: I just want to check a couple of details.

CHUNG: Of course. I don't know what I was thinking. Instinct.

He hands over the papers. WERTHEIM *reads.*

What was it in particular, perhaps I could clarify?

I'm sorry about earlier. Was my German bad?

WERTHEIM: Oh, I'd say it was pretty accurate.

CHUNG: My accent.

WERTHEIM: Clear as a bell.

CHUNG: As I mentioned, Mr Wertheim, the instructions to acquire the rabbits came from the very highest place in my country and I was instructed in no uncertain terms to acquire the rabbits really, well, really at any cost, Mr Wertheim, so if payment is the issue we can sort that out, but I really should stress that my only instructions, my only limitations on this brief were to acquire the rabbits at any cost and by any means necessary.

WERTHEIM: I see.

CHUNG: By absolutely any means necessary.

> *Slight pause.*

I do not want to leave here without the rabbits. It's not really an option for me, Mr Wertheim. I'm sure you understand. As you said so clearly, previously, you *understand*.

But if—I'm sure I could—as you mentioned, a photograph. Would a weekly photograph be sufficient?

WERTHEIM: I'd say fortnightly would do it.

> *He hands the paper over.* CHUNG *takes it but* WERTHEIM *does not let go.*

A photograph once a fortnight.

CHUNG: Of course.

> WERTHEIM *lets go of the paper. The car horn again.*

WERTHEIM: Right-o then. I'll help you with—

CHUNG: I'd say they'd have them loaded up by now.

WERTHEIM: Well, hold on, how did you get into the hutch, I—?

CHUNG: In the interests of expediency, Mr Wertheim, it has all been taken care of. There should be money in there to cover any damage to the property.

WERTHEIM: You're strangers, they won't know it's safe, they'll be frightened! I don't know how you behave in your medieval backwater police state but here you have to show people some respect!

CHUNG: With respect, Mr Wertheim, you've got what you want, now shut up and count your money. You signed the papers. The rabbits no longer belong to you.

WERTHEIM: But I raised them, I brought them up—

CHUNG: And you sold them. Just now, Mr Wertheim, you sold them. They're no longer your property.

WERTHEIM: Well, maybe I don't want to sell them after all if this is how you're going to treat them!

CHUNG: That would be stupid.

WERTHEIM: I'm sure there are plenty of people who would be interested in this shady little deal.

CHUNG: The confidentiality clause, Mr Wertheim. It would be very stupid to break that clause.

WERTHEIM: Well, it's stupid to be rude to the person you're doing business with, so it's your stupidity that will have started the chain of—

CHUNG: Do you really not get it?

WERTHEIM: You can't just—

CHUNG pulls out a gun.

CHUNG: Shut up.

Pause.

Take off your clothes.

Take them off.

WERTHEIM does.

Leave the underpants. I don't want to see your dirty German arse. Kneel down. All fours. Now pretend you're a rabbit.

Slight pause.

Do it.

WERTHEIM pretends to be a rabbit.

Hop around. More. You're a happy little rabbit.

Rabbits don't talk, Mr Wertheim. They keep their stupid mouths shut or they get whacked on the head with a shovel and thrown in the incinerator.

Learn to be a rabbit.

CHUNG *spits on him.*

You don't understand. Piece of shit.

CHUNG *goes.*

SCENE TWO

The next day, WERTHEIM, *still partly undressed, sits in the same chair with a rifle across his knees. The schnapps bottle is empty and overturned.* SOFIE AMSEL *'s voice, offstage.*

AMSEL: Hello? Mr Wertheim? Johann? The door was open, I—

AMSEL *enters.*

Oh God, don't shoot, don't shoot! It's just me, it's just Sofie, from the pet food store! You hadn't come in for days and I worried, I started to worry that maybe something had happened to the rabbits, to Felix. Mr Wertheim? Please don't shoot me. I didn't mean to interrupt you.

Pause.

Sofie. We have met before. Spoken at length on several occasions.

WERTHEIM: I know who you are.

AMSEL: I was just concerned, Mr Wertheim. I'm sorry to trespass. Maybe you could put the gun down. Or put some clothes on. Or maybe lower the gun first. Or we can—the other way round, I mean if—hey, we're simpatico, it is warm in here, look I can just, look, I'm taking my top off too, we can all be—

WERTHEIM: Keep your clothes on.

AMSEL: Okay. Why have you got a gun, Mr Wertheim?

WERTHEIM: For shooting foxes.

AMSEL: But why are you sitting inside on an armchair with a gun across your lap? Have you stuck the blinds to the windows with electrical tape?

WERTHEIM: I've taken certain precautions.

AMSEL: Precautions, Mr Wertheim? Why?

WERTHEIM: There are... I... I'm not sure that it's safe for us to speak here.

AMSEL: Why wouldn't it be safe, Mr Wertheim? This is your home.

WERTHEIM: Did you see anyone on your way here?

AMSEL: No.

WERTHEIM: Any vehicles, any suspicious vehicles parked nearby?

AMSEL: No, none, none at all. Mr Wertheim, is there something I should know about the rabbits? I know that you got them to grow very large and if you've been caught up in a steroid racket, an illegal steroid ring, I promise I won't tell, I only came out here to make sure the rabbits are alright.

WERTHEIM: I would never—

AMSEL: I know, I know, I wouldn't think that of you for a moment, but I just, I'm just struggling to make sense of all this. Where are the rabbits? Has something happened to them? Why didn't you come to us? We've got the vet next door, they said that you hadn't been in.

WERTHEIM: Felix is gone.

AMSEL: Gone, how?

WERTHEIM: Someone took him. They took them all.

AMSEL: Took them?

WERTHEIM: All of them.

AMSEL: Who could do such a thing?

WERTHEIM: Chung.

AMSEL: Who?

WERTHEIM: Mr Chung.

AMSEL: I'll call the police, we can take down a description!

WERTHEIM: No! No, you can't involve them.

AMSEL: What are you talking about? Of course you must, Mr Wertheim, I know how much those rabbits mean to you, you wouldn't part with them for anything.

WERTHEIM: It's done, Sofie, it's done. There's nothing I can do about it.

She sees the briefcase. She looks at WERTHEIM. *She goes over to the briefcase, opens it, stares at all the money.*

AMSEL: How much is there?

WERTHEIM: One hundred thousand euros.

AMSEL: I've never seen so much money. Oh, that's weird. That's weird, isn't it?! Oh, it makes my mind go all funny thinking that that's— and just there, too, just lying there! A hundred thousand—God, that's weird. Can I touch it?

WERTHEIM *nods.*

A hundred thousand euros.

Slight pause.

Just call him up and tell him that there's been a mistake.

WERTHEIM: What?

AMSEL: This Chung person. Just call him and say thank you very much for the offer, but you've changed your mind, you can't sell the rabbits, and offer to refund the money. You haven't spent any of it, have you?

WERTHEIM: No.

AMSEL: Then there's no trouble, just do an exchange.

WERTHEIM: He won't exchange them.

AMSEL: Why not?

WERTHEIM: The rabbits weren't for him, they were for someone else, he was acting under orders.

AMSEL: Orders? From whom?

WERTHEIM: I've already said too much, Sofie!

The phone begins to ring.

AMSEL: Is that them?

WERTHEIM: Probably just my mother.

AMSEL: There must be something that we can do. An anonymous tip-off to the police.

WERTHEIM: We can't go to the police, I've broken sanctions.

AMSEL: Sanctions? Who bought the rabbits, Johann?

WERTHEIM: Kim Jong-il.

AMSEL: Who?

WERTHEIM: Kim Jong-il stole my rabbits.

AMSEL: Oh.

WERTHEIM: They could be back any minute to finish me off.

AMSEL: Johann, how did you get involved with these people?

WERTHEIM: They just called. I was home. They said someone was going to pay me a visit.

AMSEL: Did they offer any proof that they were from North Korea?

WERTHEIM: He showed me his passport—his real one, not the Chinese one he came here on. I shouldn't be telling you this.

AMSEL: Johann, listen. These are serious people. If we're going to get those rabbits back we have to think like serious people as well, and you need to start by telling me everything.

WERTHEIM: Sofie, this has nothing to do with you, you should stay out of it.

AMSEL: How can I, Johann? I know those rabbits. I've seen them grow up. Every time you would bring Felix into the pet-food store, there he would be, with his wet nose and hopelessly oversized incisors. I've heard how they treat people in that country, I'm willing to bet that the treatment for rabbits isn't much better. Animals are my life, Johann. I can't just sit by while they're mistreated. Do they have an embassy?

WERTHEIM: I don't think so. It all seemed pretty underground. I wouldn't be surprised if they've been smuggled out of the country.

AMSEL: This happened last night?

WERTHEIM: Yes.

AMSEL: They won't have flown out by plane. Taking that many giant rabbits through the airport would attract too much attention. I think they will have taken them over the border into Poland, from there to Belarus, and then on a plane to North Korea.

WERTHEIM: Sofie, it's done. I sold the rabbits. They're starting a breeding program to feed their people.

AMSEL: Is that what they told you, Johann?

WERTHEIM: Yes.

AMSEL: But what if that's just what they told you?

What if it's a lie?

WERTHEIM: What can I do? Of course I want to get them back, but these are dangerous people!

AMSEL: Just contact them, at least! You must still have a contact, someone! Someone they told you to get in touch with if you needed to contact them.

WERTHEIM: Sofie, stop.

AMSEL: I've got it!

WERTHEIM: What?

AMSEL: We need to get in touch with some Christians.

WERTHEIM: Why?

AMSEL: The Bible is outlawed in North Korea. Christians have some of the best smuggling routes in and out of the country. They'll be our ticket out of there once we've secured the rabbits.

WERTHEIM: What about getting into North Korea?

AMSEL: That's the easy part! You just need to call your contact and tell them that the rabbits will die. Their selective breeding has left them with specific medical problems that only you know how to fix. You and your assistant will both need to see the rabbits.

WERTHEIM: My assistant?

AMSEL: Me, Johann.

WERTHEIM: Sofie, this is—

AMSEL: Johann, I don't mean to be rude but everyone in the village knows that you don't have any visitors, guests, ever. You live alone here, hardly leave the property except to pick up supplies for the rabbits. I know a bit about loneliness, Johann, about what it can do to a person. What will you do, all alone out here without your rabbits?

WERTHEIM: Go home, Sofie. Go home and don't come back here. Forget you ever heard about this. Perhaps they don't talk about this in the village, when they talk about me, when you talk about me, but I live alone here because I want to be alone, Sofie, I don't want to be near you, I don't care about you, any of you, I can't stand you.

He goes for the schnapps bottle.

AMSEL: It's empty.

WERTHEIM: *Get out!*

> *Pause.* AMSEL *goes. Pause for a moment as* WERTHEIM *looks after her. Then he picks up the phone and dials.*

It's Wertheim. I want to talk.

SCENE THREE

Belarus. FELIX *is sitting in an airport lounge.* CHUNG *enters.*

CHUNG: Are you comfortable?

> FELIX *nods.*

Not too hungry? I think I'll keep speaking to you in German. More familiar for you and practice for me.

FELIX: Probably a good idea. My Korean's pretty scratchy.

CHUNG: Do you want a drink? I could get you something from the cafe. Can you believe they only have one cafe in this entire airport?

FELIX: Maybe just a water.

CHUNG: Not a coffee? Isn't that the sort of thing you drink here?

FELIX: Nah, my digestive system's not really sophisticated enough to take it.

CHUNG: Oh.

FELIX: So do you do a lot of this?

CHUNG: A lot of what?

FELIX: You know. Espionage. Acquiring things of interest for your government.

CHUNG: This is my first time abroad, actually.

FELIX: Really?

CHUNG: I probably shouldn't tell you that, but there's something quite disarming about you.

FELIX: It's because evolutionarily I'm completely unequipped to be aggressive. I mean I could give you a bit of a kick with my hind legs, it might scratch a little, but really they're pretty useless. There's so much meat on me I actually find it pretty difficult to get around.

CHUNG: That could be it.

FELIX: It must be boring for your goons, carrying me everywhere. I know I'm hefty.

CHUNG: They're happy to do it.

FELIX: Yeah well, they don't sound happy. Like I said, my Korean's pretty scratchy but I know a curse word when I hear one. But that's by the by. For your first time abroad you're handling it really well.

CHUNG: Thank you.

FELIX: I've been to Poland before, to go to a rabbit show. I won first prize.

CHUNG: Well, done.

FELIX: It's just because I'm big. There was no display of skill or anything like that. I might as well have been a pumpkin. Do you want a seat? We've got a bit of time before the flight, yeah?

CHUNG: Yes.

FELIX: So have a seat, Dae-hyun. I'll shove over a bit.

CHUNG: Thank you.

> CHUNG *sits next to* FELIX.

FELIX: Is it warm in Korea this time of year?

CHUNG: No. It's cold. Similar latitude. We're a bit further south than Germany.

FELIX: I was worried that I might get a bit stuffy in my winter coat.

I'm a bit apprehensive about all this, to tell you the truth. Is that normal, do you think?

CHUNG: Oh yes, I would say so.

FELIX: All I've ever really known is my hutch. There was that trip to Poland, and once into the city for a news story, but that's really been it. So this is all pretty overwhelming. Don't get me wrong, it's wonderful, I never thought I'd get to see Belarus, let alone Korea! But here I am. I'm really going to see the world! You know, Dae-hyun, sometimes, late at night, when the frost was beginning to settle on the floor of the barn, me and the others would bunch up right up against the edge of our hutches to get close. The chicken wire would press through our fur and be so cold against our skin, but we wouldn't care. And we'd talk about what things might be like outside the barn. We'd picked up bits and pieces, like if we went to the vet and they talked about something there, or something Johann might have said. We knew enough to begin to be able to imagine the rest. And we'd laugh and make things up and our breath would be making little clouds it was so cold. And it was fun, I guess. I could see the others laughing. But it always made me sad. Because it made me think that I'll never see these places. I'll never get beyond this hutch, not really. I might get a glimpse of the sky or another animal as we drove into town but never really—

CHUNG: Well, you don't know if you'll like it in North Korea yet.

FELIX: I guess.

CHUNG: It's a long flight. We'll probably sedate you.

FELIX: Okay.

CHUNG: And you'll have to go into the cage. Just for the flight.

FELIX: What about when we land?

CHUNG: Oh, Felix. That will be different. In the DPRK, all rabbits roam free. You will be given a private meadow, with plentiful dandelion flowers whose bulbs will nourish you as never before. You and your brothers and sisters are honoured guests of our Dear Leader.

FELIX: I hope there won't be a big welcoming committee. I don't really like loud noises.

CHUNG: Oh, no. There will be some people in attendance, but I imagine it will be quite private.

Faintly, an announcement in Belarusian can be heard.

FELIX: Is that our plane?

CHUNG: Not for another hour. I could get you a magazine or—
FELIX: I think I'll just watch the people.
CHUNG: Alright.

> CHUNG's *mobile phone starts to ring.*

Do you mind if I—?
FELIX: Oh, by all means.

> CHUNG *answers.*

CHUNG: Yes. What does he say? Medical problems, what—? [*To* FELIX]
Excuse me, Felix.
FELIX: Sure.

> CHUNG *moves away from* FELIX.

CHUNG: Tell him it is impossible, that the rabbits have already been
flown—what? Yes, I know he is probably lying but—I don't see that
we have a choice. Are you sure he is acting alone? I am willing to take
the risk. Even the chance he might be telling the truth. This can't go
wrong, or it's…

I can handle it. Bring him in through China. And keep it quiet.

> CHUNG *hangs up.*

FELIX: Everything alright?
CHUNG: Yes, yes.
FELIX: You look stressed.
CHUNG: I do not, I'm not… stressed. Everything is fine.
FELIX: I'm a good listener if you need to talk. These ears aren't just for
show.
CHUNG: Thank you, Felix, but I'm fine. I'm just fine.

SCENE FOUR

North Korea. A hotel room. WERTHEIM *is standing there, with luggage.*
PARK CHUN-HEI, *a woman in her mid fifties, dressed in a North Korean
army uniform, is with him.*

PARK: Welcome to the Democratic People's Republic of Korea. My name
is Park Chun-hei, I will be your guide during your stay in the DPRK.
It is an honour to meet you, Mr Wertheim.

WERTHEIM: Pleased to meet you, Ms Park. Excuse me, I'm a little jet-lagged.

PARK: There will be plenty of time to rest. We want your stay to be relaxing and enjoyable. As an honoured guest, you will of course be given a tour of the capital. I hear that on the flight you expressed some interest in the film studio? We would be happy to arrange a visit for you.

WERTHEIM: That would be—yes, that would be lovely at some point.

PARK: Are you happy with your hotel room?

WERTHEIM: Yes, it's—

PARK: Just call the reception if you have any queries.

WERTHEIM: Is there anyone else staying here?

PARK: Excuse me?

WERTHEIM: It's a forty-floor building, but I haven't seen any other guests.

PARK: It's a new hotel, Mr Wertheim, we selected it for its proximity to the rabbit enclosure. I hope it will be acceptable.

WERTHEIM: Yes, of course.

PARK: And I must ask for your passport and any mobile phone devices.

WERTHEIM: Oh.

PARK: These are not permitted in the DPRK.

WERTHEIM: Oh.

He hands them over.

PARK: Also if you have brought a camera—

WERTHEIM: No. I left in a hurry.

PARK: Excellent. These will be kept secure until the time of your departure. Tomorrow of course you will attend to the rabbits. Then, afterwards, perhaps you would like to visit the International Friendship Exhibition Hall. We can take you there after you see the *Pueblo*, the naval ship we captured from the American imperialists in the Juche 59.

WERTHEIM: What?

PARK: 1968 in your calendar.

WERTHEIM: Yes, certainly. This is my first time in North—in the Democratic People's Republic, I would be interested to see the sights.

PARK: Of course, it will all be arranged.

WERTHEIM: Thank you, Ms Park. Do you know when I will see Mr Chung?

PARK: Who?

WERTHEIM: The man who collected the rabbits from me. Mr Chung. When will I see him again?

PARK: I don't know the person to whom you are referring, Mr Wertheim.

WERTHEIM: Oh.

PARK: There is an expert team caring for the rabbits. They have been guided directly by instructions from the Dear Leader, and you will meet with them and discuss the rabbits tomorrow morning. I will have to ask that you do not leave the hotel without an escort. You might get lost.

WERTHEIM: There seems to be hardly anyone around.

PARK: Everyone is at work, Mr Wertheim. There are jobs for all in the DPRK, and all able-bodied people are gainfully employed towards the glory of the state.

WERTHEIM: Of course. Ms Park—

PARK: Yes?

WERTHEIM: I come from a country that for a long time was divided, like yours. Do you think Korea will ever be reunited?

PARK: Of course. We are trying to reunify the country as quickly as possible.

WERTHEIM: Oh, I—

PARK: We have the leader, we have the army, we have the party. Of course reunification will occur.

WERTHEIM: Once the famine is dealt with?

PARK: There is no famine.

WERTHEIM: I thought that was why the rabbits—

PARK: The rabbits will add to the glory of the People's Republic. They will of course in the long term be used to create food security for the Korean people, but no-one ever goes hungry in the DPRK, Mr Wertheim. The care of the people is of the utmost importance to the Dear Leader.

WERTHEIM: Yes, I didn't mean to—

PARK: It's a common misunderstanding among outsiders.

WERTHEIM: Yes. I can imagine.

PARK: But I'm sure you will see, Mr Wertheim. In one week it is the birthday of the Dear Leader.

WERTHEIM: Of Kim Jong-il?

PARK: Please, please call him the Dear Leader, it is—

WERTHEIM: Oh—

PARK: For respect.

WERTHEIM: What about, um—the father, Kim Il-sung, what do I call—?

PARK: He is the Great Leader, Eternal President of the DPRK.

WERTHEIM: But isn't he—I mean he's… dead.

PARK: He is our Eternal President.

WERTHEIM: Right.

PARK: You will see on the Dear Leader's birthday, Mr Wertheim. There will be great feasts and celebrations across the nation. You will see how plentiful the land of the DPRK is. Is there anything else, Mr Wertheim?

WERTHEIM: Yes, I was hoping to ask this of Mr Chung—

PARK: Any questions you have can be directed to me.

WERTHEIM: I was wondering… you see I've been considering what the rabbits mean to me and, and the way in which the deal was made. That is to say I was a little apprehensive about the whole enterprise by the time Mr Chung and I had finished our… conversation, and I have some… concerns and, well, a request.

PARK: What is this request? I can assure you that the rabbits are extremely, extremely important to the Dear Leader.

We're very glad to have you here with us, Mr Wertheim. If I may be frank, you should have been invited here from the outset—the rabbits are your work, after all. Please let me formally apologise for any previous misunderstandings. It's a source of personal regret for me that you did not accompany the rabbits here. I'm sure our rabbit team will benefit immeasurably from your expertise. I must tell you that they are all very excited to meet the brilliant Johann Wertheim!

WERTHEIM: Oh. Well, I'm excited as well, to see how it's all coming along. Not every day that you get to be a part of something like this!

PARK: Not just a part of it, I think, Mr Wertheim. This began with you. We would not be here without you. I think we will be able to accomplish great things together.

WERTHEIM: Great things. Yes.

PARK: I'll leave you to get some rest. Our work begins tomorrow, Mr Wertheim!

WERTHEIM: Yes. I'm looking forward to it. Thank you, Ms Park.

SCENE FIVE

An office room in North Korea. PARK *and* CHUNG.

PARK: How did you find Germany?

CHUNG: Have you ever been there?

PARK: No.

CHUNG: I find that surprising.

PARK: I was about to go there when I was younger, it had been my area of training, you know, but then the Wall came down and that was that.

CHUNG: It's a decadent society. I know that Westerners are fat but it comes as a real shock, the scale of it.

PARK: The mass of it.

CHUNG: Yeah. Some remnants of the socialist state remain, but they're hard to recognise.

PARK: You saw the Wall?

CHUNG: Yeah.

PARK: Stood where the Wall used to be?

CHUNG: One foot one side, one foot the other. I took a photo.

PARK: I imagine it's quite touristy now.

CHUNG: Oh yeah, lots of tourists, but it's like a scar, really, isn't it? Still present.

PARK: What about those castles they have there, in Bavaria, did you see any of them?

CHUNG: I didn't have the opportunity. I was only in Bonn and briefly in Berlin. Almost no security! I walked right up to the Bundestag. I was on a Chinese passport of course, nothing suspect, but even so, I half-expected—you know how you always expect the—

PARK: —the worst thing—

CHUNG: Yes, exactly, the worst possible thing, but it didn't happen.

PARK: Nothing at all went wrong.

CHUNG: It was like clockwork. Not the slightest hitch.

PARK: Except that the rabbit breeder has now followed you here.

CHUNG: That was unavoidable.

PARK: It was avoidable, Chung, it was entirely avoidable, I can think of a number of ways in which it could have been avoided.

CHUNG: You have really never been there?

PARK: No.

CHUNG: And you weren't selected to go on this occasion. I was surprised, really—

PARK: No-one should have gone on this occasion. If you had reported to me as you're supposed to, I wouldn't have allowed it. It was frivolous, and very risky.

CHUNG: I was acting on the express wishes of the Dear Leader.

PARK: I'm your direct superior. You should have requested permission from me. People don't like it when the chain of command gets blurry, Chung, and I know that you understand that, you're not naïve, much as you might like to pretend to be when it suits you.

CHUNG: Comrade Park, I was ordered directly by one superior to yourself to acquire the rabbits. Should I have disobeyed?

PARK: I know damn well that it was your idea, that it was your suggestions that prompted the order. You want to make a name for yourself. I know how it is. You want some adulation, for everyone to turn around and say, 'Look how clever this one is'. It's an unhealthy instinct. Especially in someone with your tendency to leave loose ends untied.

CHUNG: I only wanted to do something for my country. For the Dear Leader. Of course I wanted to do something of note. Something that was important. Isn't that what we all want? Nothing great comes without risk.

I misjudged Wertheim's attachment to the rabbits. I admit that. My understanding of Westerners lead me to believe that we just needed to pay him enough. I didn't expect him to value the rabbits more than the money. But it's under control now.

PARK: The rabbit breeder won't be a problem. We'll allow him to tend to his rabbits, and then we will send him home. That will be the end of it.

CHUNG: Yes. I know how capable you are with these sorts of things.

PARK: With cleaning up other people's messes. Do you think I enjoy cleaning up after people, Chung?

CHUNG: No.

PARK: Well, you're wrong, I do. I really enjoy it. Because I am very good at it. And every time it gives me a little thrill, because I get to discover the weaknesses and imperfections of everyone around me, which can be very, very satisfying.

You're to have no contact with Wertheim.

CHUNG: I can fix this myself, I want to fix this myself.

PARK: I've just given you an order.

CHUNG: I understand.

PARK: And the rabbits are no longer your responsibility.

CHUNG: But—

PARK: What? You've done your part, comrade. You acquired the rabbits, exactly as requested. And now I am instructing you to stay away. Is that understood?

CHUNG: Yes.

PARK: I had my first look at the rabbits this morning. Hideous things. Ugly, stupid black eyes. Horrid teeth and spittle everywhere. Great, clumsy paws. How could anyone devote his life to anything so hideous? That is what capitalist decadence does to the mind. Wertheim must be mad.

CHUNG: Yes. I believe he is.

PARK: Aren't they hideous, Chung?

CHUNG: Yes. They disgust me.

SCENE SIX

Wertheim's room, night. Someone is rummaging through a bag.

WERTHEIM: Is someone there?

I can hear you. I can hear you breathing. So just… if you're here to spy on me or to kill me or—I guess you would have done that by now. If you're an elite killer. An assassin. Or a mercenary.

The person moves.

I'm standing in front of the door so you won't be able to get out.

AMSEL: Fuck.

WERTHEIM: Sofie?

AMSEL: Um… yes, actually. Hello, Johann.

WERTHEIM *turns on the light.*

Surprise.

WERTHEIM: What are you doing here?

AMSEL: I couldn't let you do it alone, Johann, I just couldn't! I know you didn't want me to come but I kept thinking about those poor rabbits and I just—I had to!

WERTHEIM: What are you doing in my room?

AMSEL: I didn't have anywhere to stay. It's not like I know anyone in North Korea, Johann, and I spent all my money trying to get here.

WERTHEIM: How did you get into the country?

AMSEL: I flew into China, got myself to Shenyang, bribed the staff at the North Korean consulate, officials both sides of the border, got across the border and here I am. I got to Pyongyang in the back of a truck full of chickens. I stink of shit and I'm terrified I've got lice. Can I use your shower?

WERTHEIM: What have you got behind your back?

AMSEL: Oh, this? I knocked over your bag, I was just putting it back on your desk. Sorry. I think I spilt some of your papers.

WERTHEIM: How did you get into my room?

AMSEL: The door was open.

WERTHEIM: But I made sure to—

AMSEL: Johann, I've come all this way, please, I'm exhausted. Can we talk about this in the morning?

WERTHEIM: I'm meant to be here alone.

AMSEL: No-one saw me.

WERTHEIM: I won't be able to hide you. The room is probably bugged! If they find you—it's both our necks on the line, Sofie!

AMSEL: I thought you'd be glad to see me. I came all this way to help you, Johann.

WERTHEIM: You've put us both in very serious danger, Sofie.

AMSEL: Johann, you're in the most unscrupulous and volatile dictatorship in the world, you were already in danger, I really don't see that this adds much to it. Maybe I'll even be able to help you.

WERTHEIM: How?

AMSEL: I know where they're keeping Felix.

WERTHEIM: What use is that?

AMSEL: How will we rescue him if we don't know where he is?

WERTHEIM: I'm not going to steal Felix, Sofie. Now that I'm here, perhaps I can make some good from this situation. Maybe Chung was a bit of a loose cannon, but the person I'm speaking to now, Park, seems very helpful and genuine. They've said I can be a part of setting up the breeding program here. I'm going to check on the rabbits tomorrow, and believe me, if things aren't up to scratch I'm taking my rabbits and going straight home. But if it comes to that, I'm going to buy them back.

AMSEL: Do you really think they're going to sell? Really, deep down, do you believe that? What if they say no? Are you just going to give up and go home after coming all this way? Felix can't mean all that much to you.

WERTHEIM: Don't tell me what Felix means to me. Nothing matters more to me than seeing Felix reach his full potential. If you knew how long, how hard I have worked to—

AMSEL: The North Koreans won't let you stay here forever, you know. They'll learn what they need to from you, and then it will be time for you to leave. You're kidding yourself if you think otherwise.

WERTHEIM: Well then, when I leave here, I will have been part of setting up the most sophisticated rabbit-breeding program in the world! What have you ever done? What can you claim, ever, to have achieved? I'll tell you. Nothing. Maybe by the time I have to go they'll even let me take some of my rabbits back. I think you're being very quick to judge, Sofie.

Now you can hide here, but you have to stay very quiet, and you don't do anything, anything at all. I'll find a way to let them know you're here, but until then they cannot see you, Sofie, if I lose their trust then we're—

AMSEL: I know. I'm not stupid. I can see how they're playing you.

You'll have nothing to take with you when you go. What will you do, Johann, if you go back empty-handed? What will you do with your days if every one of your rabbits stays here, on the other side of the earth?

WERTHEIM: Don't you worry about me, Sofie. I've got everything under control.

SCENE SEVEN

An indoor rabbit enclosure. WERTHEIM *and* FELIX.

WERTHEIM: How's the food?

FELIX: It's great. I can feel myself putting on weight, though. And it would be nice to be able to get out into the sunlight a bit, but I'd feel a bit churlish asking, you know. I think I'd be pushing it a bit.

WERTHEIM: Would you like me to ask?

FELIX: No, no, please don't—then they'll know it's me who's asking, but it'd be like I just wasn't brave enough to ask myself so I've got you to do it. It would be too embarrassing.

WERTHEIM: No, you should be—they should be looking after you.

FELIX: It's okay, Johann. I'll ask myself if it starts to get to me too much.

WERTHEIM: And you've got plenty of hay? Alfalfa? I hope the vegetables they're getting you are fresh.

FELIX: Yeah, yeah.

WERTHEIM: And I mean they seem to have… created a stimulating environment for you.

FELIX: I know, right? Look at all my toys. I got this great one. Here, take a look.

He shows WERTHEIM *a slinky.*

How great is this?! What's it called?

WERTHEIM: A slinky.

FELIX: Yeah, a slinky. Look at all its colours! And you know the best thing—if you put it at the top of some stairs and set it up in the right way, it'll walk down the stairs!

WERTHEIM: Right.

FELIX: Yeah, and it's just physics, there's nothing more to it than that. It's brilliant. And good to chew on as well, it's quite hardy so it's good exercise for my teeth.

WERTHEIM: You seem happy.

FELIX: Can't complain. They're treating me pretty nicely. I don't think I've ever been so pampered in my life! Oh, sorry.

WERTHEIM: No, it's alright.

FELIX: Don't get me wrong, I love it back home. And I miss the sounds, and the straw in my hutch. I do miss it, Johann.

WERTHEIM: No, I understand. It's exciting being in a new place. I'm enjoying it myself.

FELIX: That's great. Have you seen much of the country?

WERTHEIM: Not yet. They said that they would take me on a bit of a tour later on. I wanted to see you first.

FELIX: Yeah, I keep asking them about a tour but I haven't made any headway yet.

WERTHEIM: Maybe the logistics of it—

FELIX: Yeah, maybe. Anyway. Next time you come, make sure to tell me about it. Are you allowed to take photos?

WERTHEIM: I don't think so. I forgot my camera in any case.

FELIX: Too bad. Did you hear about the celebrations they're going to have for the Dear Leader's birthday? It sounds pretty spectacular. It's a shame you forgot your camera.

WERTHEIM: I suppose you must wonder why I let this happen.

FELIX *doesn't respond.*

It wasn't because I wanted to let you go, Felix, any of you. I can promise you that.

FELIX: I know.

WERTHEIM: I just… I was just in a very difficult position, you see I'd run out of money and, and—

FELIX: I get it, Johann.

WERTHEIM: But I've realised, I've realised that I should have handled this all better, I should at least have come with you and seen to it that you settled in alright, I should have insisted on that.

FELIX: It was pretty scary. That morning when they were packing us into the van. They were grabbing at us and we were screaming, these strangers with gloves shoving us into cages, I thought maybe you'd—I thought maybe you were sending us to the butcher, Johann.

WERTHEIM: No, no, I would never, Felix, never—

FELIX: But it's okay. Dae-hyun spoke to us all, calmed us down. Explained that we were going to North Korea. As honoured guests! I think some of the others thought that you were coming too, but something in me knew that we were leaving you behind, Johann.

WERTHEIM: Well, here I am!

FELIX: Yeah.

WERTHEIM: And it does seem like you're… being really looked after, so that is… a relief.

FELIX: The only weird thing is being watched all the time. I mean all the time, Johann. I wake up and there's a soldier staring at me. It's kind of awkward going to the toilet, it's just like, what, are you going to stand there and watch, and yep, they do. I'm not precious about that sort of thing, but still, it took some getting used to.

WERTHEIM: Are you happy here, though?

FELIX: What do you mean?

WERTHEIM: What if we were to go home together?

FELIX: What, go back and—and live in the barn again?

WERTHEIM: Yes. Would you want to?

Pause.

I know that the last few weeks before you left were not the best time, that there was less food than there should be, but I can promise you that it would be different this time.

FELIX: I don't know, Johann.

WERTHEIM: Think about it.

PARK *enters.*

PARK: Mr Wertheim?

WERTHEIM: Yes.

PARK: How are you getting on?

WERTHEIM: Well, thank you, Ms Park. Felix seems to be in good shape.

PARK: What do you think of the facilities?

WERTHEIM: State of the art, Ms Park, state of the art.

PARK: As you can see, all care has been taken. The site is also bomb-proofed in case of an attack by the American imperialist aggression forces who may wish to steal or destroy the rabbits.

WERTHEIM: I doubt that the Americans would have any interest in—

PARK: We are ready to respond. The state is a weapon. Every citizen is a soldier.

WERTHEIM: Yes, I'm sure.

PARK: If I may say so, Mr Wertheim?

WERTHEIM: Yes?

PARK: They are exquisite specimens. The rabbits. Quite miraculous. They are a testament to your vision.

WERTHEIM: Thank you, Ms Park.

PARK: Well, if you have finished here, Mr Wertheim, it's time to go.

WERTHEIM: I haven't seen them all yet.

PARK: There will be time for that later. We are running late.

Slight pause.

FELIX: Go on, Johann, I'll be fine.
WERTHEIM: Alright. I'll see you very soon, Felix.
FELIX: Sure.

>   PARK *escorts* WERTHEIM *away.*

Bye.

SCENE EIGHT

A public square in Pyongyang. CHUNG *is there.* AMSEL *enters.*

AMSEL: Hello, Dae-hyun.
CHUNG: What are you doing here?
AMSEL: They brought me in. Didn't you know?
CHUNG: I—of course I—
AMSEL: I didn't realise you were so far out of the loop these days.
CHUNG: That will change.
AMSEL: Maybe.
CHUNG: You're my asset, you shouldn't be brought in without my say-so.
AMSEL: My cover was threatened. You wouldn't want anyone to get a hold of me, would you? Not with the information I've got.
CHUNG: You know less than you think, Amsel.
AMSEL: Oh, almost certainly. But that's still enough.
CHUNG: Does Wertheim know you're here?
AMSEL: Of course. We have to make him think that I'm here to assist him. If he saw me here and didn't know why I was here, well, my cover would definitely be blown and I'd be no use to you at all. He thinks I'm hiding in his room. It's useful; this way we can keep an eye on Wertheim at all times, and I can stay away from Germany until the heat's off. It wasn't easy for me to facilitate your visit to Germany, you know, not without risk, so a 'thank you' wouldn't go astray.

How did you like your time there?
CHUNG: It's a strange place.
AMSEL: Yes. It's been corrupted so quickly. The American imperialists have put their stamp on the country. Even in the east there's almost no-one who fights for true socialism anymore.
CHUNG: I want you to update me on—
AMSEL: I'm reporting to Park Chun-hei.

CHUNG: Of course.

AMSEL: So if you want to know anything you'll have to talk to her. I know there's no love lost between you—

CHUNG: My relationship with comrade Park is completely professional, Ms Amsel. You should be cautious. No asset is indispensable.

AMSEL: That a threat, Dae-hyun?

Pause.

So tell me then: why all the fuss over these rabbits?

CHUNG: The Dear Leader expressed an interest in them, and so I took it upon myself to acquire them.

AMSEL: So this is your little pet project?

CHUNG: I was acting upon the Dear Leader's expressed interest.

AMSEL: Needed something to raise your stocks a bit? I bet Park wasn't too happy when she found out the rabbit breeder would be coming along for the ride.

CHUNG: I'm sure Wertheim is under control if you're keeping an eye on him, Ms Amsel.

AMSEL: But what I'm asking, Mr Chung, what I'm asking is what the Dear Leader's particular interest in the rabbits is.

CHUNG: The Dear Leader saw the pictures of the rabbits on the internet and expressed an interest in what a rabbit of that size would taste like. It was agreed that for the Dear Leader's upcoming birthday celebrations a dish of particular magnificence was required. I took it upon myself to acquire the rabbits. One has been butchered already and was found to have excellent taste. I expect that the others will be of similar quality, especially the prize specimen. Felix.

AMSEL: I see. So that famine relief program Johann mentioned—

CHUNG: A necessary fabrication.

AMSEL: Don't you think it's necessary that some steps be taken to deal with the famine?

CHUNG: That's not your concern, Amsel.

AMSEL: Not yours, either?

CHUNG: No. I hope you're not wavering in your commitment to socialism, Sofie?

AMSEL: What? No. No question.

It's hard, living among the enemy. You've never had to do it so don't presume to…

CHUNG: You look tired.

AMSEL: I'm not tired. Fuck off, Chung.

> CHUNG *shrugs.*

CHUNG: People are watching us.

AMSEL: I know.

CHUNG: You should be the one to leave. Maybe pay your respects to the Great Leader, lay a wreath at—

AMSEL: It was the first thing I did.

CHUNG: Good.

AMSEL: Did you taste the rabbit?

How did it taste?

CHUNG: I have reason to believe that the Dear Leader will be very, very pleased.

SCENE NINE

Felix's enclosure. Night-time. It's dark. FELIX *is there, apparently asleep.* PARK *is there as well, watching him.*

PARK: Felix. Are you awake? Felix?

FELIX: Who's there?

PARK: It's just me, Felix. It's Chun-hei.

FELIX: Oh, hi. I've met so many new people since coming here.

PARK: Of course. It must be quite overwhelming for a young rabbit such as yourself.

FELIX: Well, it is exciting. I wouldn't say overwhelming. Chun-hei?

PARK: Yes?

FELIX: Is there a reason that the lights are off?

PARK: Oh, no. No reason. It's just nice in the dark sometimes, don't you think?

FELIX: Well, I'm more at home in the dark. I just thought if you—

PARK: Oh, I'm fine. Don't worry about me. I like the dark as well sometimes.

FELIX: I just can't see your face that well.

PARK: That's alright. We can just talk to each other.

FELIX: What's the time?

PARK: I'm not really sure.

FELIX: It feels very late.

PARK: Oh, I'm sorry I woke you up. I didn't mean to.

FELIX: That's okay. I wasn't asleep actually. I know that you've been here for a while.

PARK: Really?

FELIX: Yeah, I could feel you watching me but I felt a bit awkward so I thought if I just pretended to be asleep that you might go away, but that was about half an hour ago I think.

PARK: Right, yes.

FELIX: Is there any particular reason that you were watching me?

PARK: No. No reason. Was it nice seeing Johann again today?

FELIX: Yeah. I guess.

PARK: I can't stay long. I have to go and look after him.

FELIX: Oh well, I don't want to keep you—

PARK: Tomorrow you'll get to go outside. We're going to take you up to the mountains above Pyongyang.

FELIX: Is that where the meadow is?

PARK: The meadow?

FELIX: Dae-hyun said something about a meadow, and plentiful dandelion bulbs. He kind of promised that they'd be waiting for us. I hadn't said anything because I didn't want to cause a fuss, but—

PARK: Dae-hyun is not a helpful person, Felix.

FELIX: Oh. But he seemed so nice.

PARK: In this world, Felix, there are people that you can't trust. People who want things from you. Difficult things. People who will hurt you.

FELIX: I'm sorry if I did anything to upset Dae-hyun, I—

She pats him.

PARK: Forget about him, Felix. You won't see him again.

She continues to stroke him.

Do you like that?

FELIX: What?

PARK: You have such beautiful fur, Felix.

FELIX: Oh. Thank you.

PARK: It's so soft.

FELIX: Well, I never got out that much, you know. Lived a pretty. Indoors. Kind of life, so… not much opportunity for it to get matted up and… I like to keep myself, you know, respectable—

PARK: Am I making you uncomfortable?

FELIX: No, no.

PARK: You don't like me touching you?

FELIX: No, I… it's nice.

PARK: What about just there? Behind the ear.

FELIX: Yes, that's nice too.

PARK: So soft.

FELIX: Well, like I said, I—

PARK: Nothing at all like my hair.

FELIX: Well, we are… different.

PARK: Feel my hair, Felix.

FELIX: Sorry?

PARK: Just put your paw on my hair. And stroke. Very gently.

> FELIX *does.*

How does that feel?

FELIX: Nice. It feels nice.

PARK: It's so cold in here. Aren't you cold?

FELIX: Well, I've still got my winter coat so I'm pretty well insulated actually.

PARK: Do you mind if I just get a bit closer?

FELIX: Oh, I—

PARK: I'm just so cold, Felix. You don't mind, do you?

FELIX: No.

PARK: I can see you better now that we're close.

FELIX: Yes.

PARK: I can see your beautiful eyes.

FELIX: Oh, I don't like my eyes.

PARK: Why not?

FELIX: I feel like they're a bit bulgy. A bit oversized, you know, on account of my narrow gene pool?

PARK: No, Felix, they're beautiful. Such beautiful dark eyes. What brilliant insight for the Dear Leader to bring you here. Soon you will meet the Dear Leader. You will have a private audience. Oh, Felix, I don't mind saying that I'm envious. To see the Dear Leader up close with your own eyes! It's a rare, such a rare privilege. One day I hope to have that privilege. It's what sustains me, Felix. That one day I might set eyes on his beautiful, blessed face. He will look into your beautiful eyes the way I am looking into them now. From the minute I saw you I thought, 'What beautiful eyes. Eyes you could fall into.'

FELIX: Yours are nice too.

PARK: Look in my eyes.

> *She kisses him. It's quite a long kiss. Then silence for a little while.*

FELIX: Wow.

PARK: You're so beautiful, Felix. So beautiful.

FELIX: Am I?

> *She kisses him again.*

Chun-hei—

PARK: What is it?

FELIX: I've never… God, this is embarrassing. I've never.

PARK: Shhh. Shhh, Felix. Come here.

> *They begin to make love.*

Yes… yes… I am so close to you… I am so close to you, my Dear Leader… I will be so close to you… what I have touched will be inside you! I will be inside you!

SCENE TEN

The hotel room. AMSEL *is there alone, waiting. She's impatient, on edge. The door opens. She hides herself.* WERTHEIM *and* PARK *can be heard.*

WERTHEIM: Thank you, Ms Park, goodnight.

PARK: Don't forget your souvenir.

WERTHEIM: Oh, yes—

PARK: Here, I'll put it on the table for you.

WERTHEIM: That's alright, I can—thank you, that's—oh look, you're coming into the room.

> PARK *enters, followed by* WERTHEIM. *She leaves a small, plain, cardboard box on the table.* WERTHEIM *looks around desperately for* AMSEL.

Thank you, that was—it was a long day, I'm very, oh, is that, look how late it is.

PARK: It's not so late. You should come downstairs later, to the bar. We can sing karaoke.

WERTHEIM: Oh, yes, that would be—

PARK: We will I'm sure have all your favourites, Beatles, Beach Boys, Michael Bolton.

WERTHEIM: Mm.

PARK: We could take the machine out to the rabbit hutches. We could sing to the rabbits.

WERTHEIM: Ha ha, that sounds, yes, that sounds like a lovely idea.

> WERTHEIM *clears his throat loudly.*

PARK: Well, I will see you downstairs later, then.

WERTHEIM: Yes, yes you will.

> PARK *goes. The door closes.*

Sofie—

> AMSEL *stands up, waves her hands, gestures furiously for* WERTHEIM *to be silent. She points at the cardboard box. She goes to her bag and takes out a small black device, then puts it next to the cardboard box. A little red light on the device indicates that it is on.* AMSEL *then switches on some music.*

AMSEL: Talk quietly.

WERTHEIM: What?

AMSEL: Talk quietly. My signal blocker should be doing the trick, but it would be good not to take too many risks. We have to be careful, Johann. We must be very, very careful. Things have changed. Developments have—changes have developed beyond our—

WERTHEIM: Sofie, what is it?

AMSEL: Don't say my name! Listen, Johann, and listen carefully, we don't have long. You're going to have to go downstairs before they get suspicious. Make sure to have a very good time. Buy people drinks. Lots of drinks. But try not to drink too much yourself. We need to be sharp. We're only going to get one opportunity.

WERTHEIM: What are you talking about?

AMSEL: In two days time it's Kim Jong-il's birthday. Do you know what they're serving up to him, Johann? Big steaks of Felix.

WERTHEIM: What? No, Felix is here for… for a breeding program, that's not—

AMSEL: Not what Mr Chung told you? Grow up, Johann. Listen to me. We're going to have a chance to be there at that feast. We can't do anything to the rabbits because Kim has a poison taster eat everything before he even touches it, so we're going to have to get within striking distance—

WERTHEIM: Striking distance?

AMSEL: Don't you get it, Johann? [*She mouths the next words.*] I'm CIA.

WERTHEIM: What?

AMSEL: I'm CIA!

WERTHEIM: Oh, God.

AMSEL: No-one's ever gotten this close. I can't believe it's me! Now listen, Johann. My people will get us out of the country, but only if you do exactly as I tell you.

WERTHEIM: They're going to—they bought them for Kim Jong-il to eat on his birthday?

They're going to kill him. What have I—we have to do something, we have to rescue them!

AMSEL: It's too late for that, Johann. Felix has to give the last full measure of devotion. There's no way around it. But it will give us a shot at Kim Jong-il.

WERTHEIM: I don't care about Kim Jong-il! And what if you're discovered, Sofie, they'll kill you, they'll kill me!

AMSEL: Listen, Wertheim, you're going through with this. Yes, the North Koreans might kill you if I fail, but I will definitely kill you if you don't help me. I've gotten too fucking close to fall short now. We'll never get another chance like this. I mean it's not strictly CIA policy and sure, I'm going slightly against my directives, but if I pull this off that won't matter!

WERTHEIM: You knew this was going to happen all along, didn't you?

AMSEL: Yeah, more or less.

WERTHEIM: And you—you used me.

AMSEL: Don't be a child, Johann, of course I used you.

WERTHEIM: But—but you're acting alone. You've got no support. You're going against your orders, they won't rescue you.

AMSEL: Oh, I don't know about that, Johann. Things change. For seven years I've been paddling around some backwater German town with fuck-all to do, shoved out of sight out of mind, not because I was bad at my job, Johann, I am good at my job, but because I offended the wrong people. But over those seven fucking years I have built up a very effective network, I knew every movement in that area, so I was perfectly placed that when opportunity came I was right there. At last! I'd been waiting for so long, playing the North Koreans for all they're worth. I have worked so fucking hard for this and now it's here. When this is over no-one's ever going to overlook me again. I am going to be a fucking hero. Now go downstairs and sing some very patriotic songs. Sing your little rabbit heart out.

SCENE ELEVEN

The rabbit enclosure. A karaoke booth has been set up. FELIX *and* WERTHEIM *are there.* PARK *is singing a song. After a little while:*

FELIX: Beautiful song, isn't it?

WERTHEIM: Yeah. Compelling.

FELIX: She's got a nice voice, too, doesn't she, Johann?

WERTHEIM: Yes.

FELIX: Earlier today they showed me—we had a visit from a primary school. These kids all lined up in a row, playing guitars. Incredible! Some of them were even smaller than the guitars. They were smiling in a kind of eerie way. You knew that if they stuffed up they would be held under a hot tap but still, it was hard not to be impressed. Are you alright, Johann?

WERTHEIM: What?

FELIX: You seem distracted.

WERTHEIM: Oh. I was… listening to the song.

FELIX: Oh, sure. We can just listen if you like.

WERTHEIM: Yeah. Yes, let's just… we'll just listen. Maybe you'll sing something later, Felix.

FELIX: Oh, no no, I'd be too embarrassed. No-one needs to hear that!

WERTHEIM: You should. You don't need to be embarrassed, it's just me here. It's good to sing.

FELIX: I guess.

> PARK *finishes her song. They applaud.*

That was excellent, Ms Park!

PARK: Thank you, Felix. I think it's your turn.

FELIX: I'm shy.

PARK: I will sing with you. We can sing a duet.

WERTHEIM: Go on.

FELIX: Okay.

> PARK *and* FELIX *sing a song. After a little while,* CHUNG *enters and sits down next to* WERTHEIM.

CHUNG: Hello.

WERTHEIM: Hello.

> *Pause.*

CHUNG: I'm sorry we parted on such bad terms.

WERTHEIM: Oh, no. No no no.

CHUNG: I hope we will be able to be friends from now on.

WERTHEIM: Mm.

CHUNG: You've been very quiet this evening.

WERTHEIM: You've been watching me.

CHUNG: Of course. That's my job, Mr Wertheim.

> *Pause.*

WERTHEIM: Ms Park sings very well.

CHUNG: I'm very impressed with Felix.

WERTHEIM: Yes, look at him! I've never seen him so happy.

> WERTHEIM *waves to* FELIX, *who waves back.*

CHUNG: Tomorrow they will be taken up to the hill above Pyongyang to taste some wild Korean grasses. We will show them the whole vista. Then in a few days, the rabbits will be guests of honour at the birthday of the Dear Leader.

WERTHEIM: Yes. Felix mentioned.

CHUNG: And I trust that you have been able to care for the rabbits, Mr Wertheim, that this unfortunate genetic predisposition to disease has been satisfactorily resolved.

WERTHEIM: Yes. It was a… relatively simple fix in the end.

CHUNG: So you will be able to go home soon.

WERTHEIM: …Yes.

CHUNG: I imagine you don't like to leave your farm unattended.

WERTHEIM: Well—

CHUNG: You can see that Felix is being excellently cared for. I hope that you have enjoyed your stay in the DPRK, but I have taken the liberty of arranging your travel home.

WERTHEIM: I had… hoped to stay until the Dear Leader's birthday. Have a chance to… pay my respects.

CHUNG: I do not think this will be possible, Mr Wertheim. It is a very private affair for the Korean people. We will have to ask you to leave before the birthday. But I am glad that you have been able to see how very well we are caring for Felix.

WERTHEIM: Yes.

CHUNG: And I have been glad of the opportunity to see you again. It's been an unexpected pleasure.

WERTHEIM: So I am… to go home.

CHUNG: Tomorrow. And you never need to think about this again.

WERTHEIM: But what about… you see… I was hoping, Mr Chung, to take Felix with me.

CHUNG: I am afraid this will not be possible. My advice to you, Mr Wertheim. And I mean this sincerely. Is to go home.

WERTHEIM: Surely you don't need them all, please, please just let me save something, let me take Felix, I don't care that there's no breeding program, I just want to take my rabbit home.

> *Slight pause.*

CHUNG: How did you come by that knowledge, Mr Wertheim?

There's something you need to tell me.

WERTHEIM: I—I can—if I tell you, I need something in return.

CHUNG: What?

WERTHEIM: You have to promise me, *promise* me, Chung, that I can go home. That I can take Felix with me. That's my price.

CHUNG: But you don't have anything that we want, Johann. We don't need any more assets in Germany, certainly not a rabbit breeder who would be constantly under suspicion due to a recent unexplained trip to North Korea.

WERTHEIM: Fine. If you don't want my information, I won't give it.

> *Pause.*

CHUNG: If it's worth it, Johann. I promise I will do everything that I can to ensure that Felix is returned to you.

Pause.

Say it.

Say it, Wertheim.

WERTHEIM: There is a woman who has smuggled herself into my apartment.

CHUNG: Oh, Johann.

He laughs.

We know all about Amsel. That is your information?

WERTHEIM: Sofie is CIA.

CHUNG: What?

WERTHEIM: She's CIA. She's here to kill Kim Jong-il.

Pause. The song finishes.

Mr Chung? What—what is it are you—?

CHUNG: She's my asset.

WERTHEIM: But—you know, now, you know. I'm not sure that she's operating under orders I think she might… I think she's—gone rogue.

CHUNG: It doesn't matter.

I'm a failure. I never should have tried. Should have just… kept my head down. Johann, I'm a failure.

Pause.

Where is she?

PARK: She's secure.

CHUNG: Park Chun-hei—

PARK: Keep silent, Chung. Mr Wertheim? You had better come with me.

WERTHEIM: Yes, alright. What will happen to Mr Chung?

PARK: You had better come with me now, Mr Wertheim.

FELIX: Johann? What's going on?

PARK: *Now*, Mr Wertheim!

WERTHEIM *begins to leave. She holds him back.*

You have been very stupid.

PARK *and* WERTHEIM *go.*

FELIX: Dae-hyun? Where are they taking Johann? What's going on? Johann?! Johann!

SCENE TWELVE

A prison cell. WERTHEIM *and* AMSEL *are there, handcuffed.* PARK *is there as well.*

PARK: You were very stupid to think that we were not aware of your plot. The Dear Leader knew of it, he looked at a photograph of you, Amsel, and could discern from it that you were not honest, that you were not pledged to the principles of socialism. We only let your plan unravel this far in order to detect if you were acting under the sanction of the American imperialists. But of course they have cut you loose. They were unhappy with you. Don't expect them to offer you any assistance. Even if you were acting under orders, you should have known that it is impossible to defeat the armies of the DPRK. We will smite all aggressors mercilessly. It would be easier on both of you if you told us everything you know immediately.

WERTHEIM: I don't know anything.

PARK: Speak only when instructed!

WERTHEIM: But I don't know anything, I'm just a rabbit farmer.

PARK: Everyone knows something, Mr Wertheim, everyone is of value. And I mean to extract every bit of information from both of you. I am going to wring you dry. I don't care how long it takes. I've got all the time in the world.

Darkness. Light. WERTHEIM *and* AMSEL *are alone.*

WERTHEIM: Sofie? Do you think they're listening to us?

AMSEL: Of course they are.

WERTHEIM: What do you think is going to happen? I've lost track of time. Has the birthday celebration happened yet?

AMSEL: Not yet.

WERTHEIM: How do you keep track of the time?

AMSEL: It's in my body, Johann. My training. They haven't broken me yet. Park tells me that you tried to double-cross me to Chung.

WERTHEIM: Yes, I did.

AMSEL: I thought you might. I didn't think you had the guts, though. Risk. Misjudged it. Right at the end. Got so… so fucking close. I could have been a fucking hero.

WERTHEIM: Oh, Sofie... oh, you're not really CIA. None of it's true. Just tell them.

AMSEL: What does it matter? I'm Clint Eastwood. I'm a fucking cowboy.

Pause.

WERTHEIM: What do you think has happened to Mr Chung?

AMSEL: Exactly what's going to happen to us, Johann.

WERTHEIM: But they can't—I mean they can't kill us. The German government, surely they will—

AMSEL: Don't be stupid, Johann. You'll have been washed downriver, or something. Drowned by accident. No-one will ask too many questions. You're not that special.

WERTHEIM: But I—I'm not ready.

AMSEL: Then use this time constructively.

WERTHEIM: I've been so stupid. I should never have taken that phone call. I should never have agreed to see Mr Chung. I was just flattered that someone was interested in my rabbits. I was flattered.

I had thought, with the rabbits, that I could create something... if not perfect, then beautiful, at least. I thought that was something worth striving for. But the truth is, Sofie, that the rabbits had become a routine. I don't know why I kept caring for them. I kept telling myself all the reasons, but time made the reasons sound hollow. I would wake up in the morning and tell myself that I was enthusiastic. Oh, another day I get to be with my rabbits, how lucky I must be that I get to spend my life in this way, how many people must dream of this, I told myself, spending all their waking hours in the company of the things they love.

Only I didn't love them anymore. They bored me. I reached the limits of my knowledge but had no-one to teach me more, and no-one was interested in sharing what I had managed to come up with. But I persisted, and my persistence in the face of hopelessness disgusted me, what a stupid fucker I must be, I thought. I hated myself for my pride in my work. What work? They were just a bunch of stupid rabbits.

I had loved them with all my heart but had no-one who would share that love. And like most things that can't be shared, that can't move, like most things that begin to pool in dark places, my love began to fester. I began to hate the rabbits for making me poor and ridiculous and alone because I had poured everything into them and no-one else gave a fuck.

So I stopped feeding them.

Who cares, let them die, I thought. Only I will know, and then they will all be dead and I can't begin again and it will all be over.

The first day they were confused, but not too distressed. As time went on, they got very thin. They began to bleat constantly. Their cries at night were horrible to listen to. I was killing them. I was killing any desire that I might have to go into that barn ever again.

After a little while I stopped hearing them. Oh, Sofie, I thought I had done it. I thought it was over at last and finally I could imagine a life without them, a small, easy life with nothing so distressing as hope ever appearing on the horizon.

And then the phone rang. It was Mr Chung with an enquiry about the rabbits. He hardly needed to say two words and I was running out to the barn to check on them, praying that it was not too late. The slightest hint of interest and I was reeled back in. Utterly, utterly pulled back in.

Maybe it would have been better if it had been too late.

How cruel it is to hope. How impossible not to.

Sofie?

AMSEL: Get some sleep, Johann.

> *Darkness. Light.*

> WERTHEIM *wakes up.* AMSEL *is not there, just her coat.*

WERTHEIM: Sofie?

> *There's no reply.*

Sofie?

> *Darkness. Light.*

> PARK *is there.*

PARK: Hello, Johann.

WERTHEIM: Ms Park.

PARK: How are you holding up?

WERTHEIM: I'm hungry.

PARK: Yes.

WERTHEIM: And I think I... I smell quite bad. It can't have been that long but I am beginning to smell and I wonder if—I wonder if you could tell me how long I've been here?

PARK *remains inscrutable.*

Where is Sofie?

What about Mr Chung?

Felix? No, don't—

I just want to go home.

Please just let me go home. I won't tell anyone. I won't tell anyone anything. You know I... I hate the USA as well. A lot of the time. What they did in South America, that's—I don't agree with a lot of their—I went to rallies against the war, the war in Iraq, I, I am a firm supporter of efforts to keep, to keep hegemony in check, I really, I really don't think it's the answer, we have, we have things in common. And I am very good at keeping quiet, I can be so quiet, quiet as a little... I'm just going to go back to my farm and live, live a very quiet life and I won't talk, not to anyone, if you don't want me to. I have had enough excitement, I don't want any more. I don't want anything more. I just want to go home. Please. Please, Ms Park. Please just let me go home. I was wrong. I was wrong. Please.

Pause. PARK *goes. Darkness.*

Light. WERTHEIM *is there alone. The sound of a door opening.* FELIX *enters, looking worse for wear. Half of his left ear has been cut off. He wears handcuffs. Silence for a little while.*

WERTHEIM: Felix?

FELIX: Who else?

WERTHEIM: Look at you. What happened to your ear?

FELIX: Oh, it's nothing, Johann. Really, I'm okay. I have pretty exceptional hearing even just with the one. Just excuse me if I tend to lean in a bit.

WERTHEIM: What have they done to you?

FELIX: Don't fuss, you'll make me feel self-conscious. We haven't got a lot of time. It's almost morning.

WERTHEIM: Is it? I've lost track of time. I don't expect ever to see the sun again.

FELIX: Oh, never say never, Johann. We can't tell what life has in store for us.

WERTHEIM: No, I suppose not.

FELIX: Have they been treating you alright?

WERTHEIM: Oh, alright. I still have my ears.

FELIX: Ha! That's a plus. That's definitely a plus.

WERTHEIM: I don't know what happened to Sofie, though.

FELIX: Oh, you didn't—they didn't tell you?

WERTHEIM: Nothing. Do you know something?

FELIX: Yeah. She killed herself. Had a pill stashed somewhere.

WERTHEIM: She—she's dead?

FELIX: Oh, yeah. At least that's what I heard. Who really knows, though? But she was ready for it, Johann. She was willing to die to achieve what she wanted. It's a dangerous way to live. She knew the risks.

WERTHEIM: Do you know what will happen to me?

> FELIX *tips his head to the side.*

FELIX: I can't see into the future, Johann.

WERTHEIM: No.

FELIX: But I think this is the last time we'll see each other.

WERTHEIM: Yes. I hadn't…

I hadn't thought that I would see you again.

FELIX: Small blessings.

WERTHEIM: Yes.

FELIX: I have something that I want to give you.

WERTHEIM: Oh.

FELIX: It's nothing much. It's just a tuft of my fur.

WERTHEIM: Oh, Felix.

FELIX: It's been falling out in chunks lately. They think it's probably stress. Here. Hold onto it, Johann. Keep it somewhere safe.

WERTHEIM: I will.

FELIX: This is all going to be over soon. It's Kim Jong-il's birthday today. They won't have any reason to keep you here after that.

> *Pause.*

Johann?

WERTHEIM: Can you forgive me?

FELIX: Forgive you for what?

WERTHEIM: All this. The way it began. The way it's turned out.

FELIX: Oh.

I don't know, Johann. I guess my life hasn't really allowed me to choose many things for myself. But that's the life of most people, really. Fitting in what choices they can while the world relentlessly decides the rest.

But I could never have imagined, Johann, when I was just a kitten, when my whole world was the barn and the straw and my mother's warm body, I could never have imagined that I would see what I've seen. I've travelled across half the world, met so many different people. I'm proud of the life I've had. None of us gets to choose when and how we die.

A knock on the door.

I think our time's up.

WERTHEIM: Okay.

FELIX: Johann?

No, I don't forgive you.

Pause. FELIX *goes. Darkness. Light.*

PARK *is there.* WERTHEIM *is asleep.*

PARK: Wake up, Mr Wertheim.

WERTHEIM: Is it time?

PARK: Yes, it's time for you to go home.

WERTHEIM: What?

PARK: It's time for you to go home, Mr Wertheim.

WERTHEIM: No…

PARK: Yes. I am sorry about the last few days. But they have been a necessary precaution. You see the Dear Leader's birthday is a large event and we must take all possible measures to ensure the security of the event. But it is over now. So you may leave. Please stand. Your plane is leaving in two hours and I imagine that you would like to shower and get a change of clothes before your flight.

WERTHEIM *begins to cry quietly.*

Time is pressing, Mr Wertheim.

WERTHEIM: It will be… so quiet at home.

PARK: You will be debriefed on the plane. I advise you not to speak to anyone of this. If I may speak frankly, Mr Wertheim, the whole enterprise was a foolish one. From start to finish. Had it been up to me none of this would have happened.

> *Slight pause.*

I feel like we haven't met one another. That we could sit in this room together for a very long time and never meet one another.

> *Pause.*

WERTHEIM: I want to go home.
PARK: Yes.

I'm sure you do.

> PARK *opens the door.*

WERTHEIM: Can you… can you tell me what happened to Mr Chung?
PARK: Who?

No such person exists.

It's time to go.
WERTHEIM: Yes. Time to go.

SCENE THIRTEEN

Wertheim's home. WERTHEIM *is there, alone.*

Some time passes.

A POSTAL EMPLOYEE *enters.*

The EMPLOYEE *carries a small cardboard box with a number of holes punched into the side of it.*

EMPLOYEE: I have a delivery.

> WERTHEIM *doesn't respond. The* EMPLOYEE *places the box on the ground.*

You have to sign for it.
WERTHEIM: Yes, alright.

> WERTHEIM *signs.*

> *The* EMPLOYEE *leaves.*

The box and WERTHEIM *watch each other.*

WERTHEIM *goes to the box. Opens it. Reaches in and pulls out a rabbit; a small, mottled mini lop.*

He lifts the rabbit and holds it at eye level.

The rabbit and WERTHEIM *watch each other for a little while.*

THE END

GRIFFIN THEATRE COMPANY PRESENTS THE WORLD PREMIERE OF

A RABBIT FOR KIM JONG-IL
BY KIT BROOKMAN

Director Lee Lewis
Designer Elizabeth Gadsby
Lighting Designer Luiz Pampolha
Composer/Sound Designer Steve Francis
Stage Manager Charlotte Barrett
With Kate Box, Kit Brookman, Kaeng Chan, Steve Rodgers, Mémé Thorne

SBW STABLES THEATRE
10 OCTOBER - 21 NOVEMBER

GRIFFIN THEATRE COMPANY

Production Sponsor

HOLDING REDLICH

Government Partners

Australian Government

Australia Council for the Arts

NSW GOVERNMENT | Arts NSW

Co-commissioned by Playwriting Australia and Griffin Theatre Company with the support of the Robertson Family Foundation.

PLAYWRIGHT'S NOTE

This play is not a true story, but it is inspired by one.

In 2006, in Germany, a breeder of giant rabbits was approached by the North Korean government to acquire a number of his rabbits, ostensibly for a breeding program to be set up in North Korea. He agreed to sell his rabbits. No one quite knows what happened next, except that his invitation to go to North Korea to oversee the creation of a rabbit-breeding program was abruptly cancelled without explanation.

How does one grapple with the idea of North Korea? The concurrent absurdity and horror of the place makes for a confusing mix. It's the world's most isolated nation, repressive at home and belligerent abroad. We're used to hearing strange stories, most of which stem from what might be called the eccentricities of its tyrannical ruling dynasty. Many of these seem too strange to be true. They defy belief.

A recent UN enquiry into atrocities committed in North Korea found that the actions of the Kim regime have caused the deaths of "at the very least hundreds of thousands of human beings." This, too, in its horrific way, defies belief. There are some crimes so large that the mind bends when it tries to comprehend the scale of their brutality.

This play, clearly, is not and does not aim to be a naturalistic representation of the events that inspired it, or of the true situation in recent times in North Korea, but that truth hovers at its shoulder as the waking world sits beside a dream, or nightmare. It is a fable about guilt and forgiveness, about the things we are willing to ignore in order to succeed, and the price we pay for having ignored them when we do.

The play was written with the assistance of Playwriting Australia and the Robertson Family Foundation, and I'm grateful for their support. It was written while I was a member of the Griffin Studio and I'd like to thank the generous donors who make that program possible. A big thank-you also to Lee Lewis for her intelligent guidance in the development of the script and for her determination to realise it. Thank you also to the actors who assisted in the play's development, the cast and creative team of this production, and everyone at Griffin.

And thanks, as always, to Luke.

Kit Brookman
Writer

DIRECTOR'S NOTE

A Rabbit for Kim Jong-il strikes at the heart of one of the great challenges of the 21st Century. Forgiveness. How do we forgive great crimes? How do we forgive the crimes of the 20th Century? How do we forgive betrayal? Do we even believe in forgiveness in a time when the faith mechanisms which promoted it are so badly eroded? In the age of selfishness is it even possible? And if it is not possible, how then do we carry the burden of our crimes as we continue to live? Can we learn from our history and change or are we fated to repeat the same mistakes in each generation?

This play does not have answers but it has big questions. It is a fable for our times. Without forgiveness what future is there for Australia? How inarticulate are we about our national crimes that we need a play set in Germany and North Korea in order to even consider them?

I would like to thank Kit Brookman for trusting Griffin with this play. I have worked with and alongside Kit for many years now; he is a very fine actor, an emerging director, and a writer of delicacy and courage. With all that talent it is fascinating how successfully he avoids the pitfalls of the wunderkind traditions.

I am looking forward to rehearsals and seeing, when the audience arrives, how ready we are to face some of the questions this play will ask.

Lee Lewis
Director

Kit Brookman

Playwright / Felix

Kit's recent work as writer includes: *Small and Tired* –
which was shortlisted for the 2012 Griffin Award and
went on to be staged at Belvoir. His play *Close* was
shortlisted for the Griffin Award in 2010 and the Patrick
White Award in 2011. Other recent work includes *Nora*
(co-written for Belvoir); *Heaven* (La Mama); *Night Maybe*
(Stuck Pigs Squealing). Kit trained as an actor at NIDA.
He has appeared on stage in *Twelfth Night*, also directed
by Lee Lewis (Bell Shakespeare), *A Midsummer Night's
Dream* (B-Sharp), *DNA* (Old Fitzroy), and on television
in *Micronation*. Kit's recent directing work includes *Is
This Thing On?* (with Zoe Coombs-Marr) which won
Best Ensemble Cast at 2014 Sydney Theatre Awards;
Small and Tired; and *Heaven* at La Mama. As assistant
director, Kit has worked on Belvoir's productions of *Cat
On a Hot Tin Roof*, *Private Lives*, and *Babyteeth*.

Lee Lewis

Director

Lee is the Artistic Director of Griffin Theatre Company. She is one of Australia's leading directors, having worked for numerous main stage companies. Lee's credits for Griffin include: *The Bleeding Tree*; *Masquerade* (co-directed with Sam Strong); *Emerald City, The Serpent's Table* (co-directed with Darren Yap), *The Bull, the Moon and the Coronet of Stars*, *A Hoax*, *Silent Disco*, *The Call* and *The Nightwatchman*; for Sydney Theatre Company: *Honour, ZEBRA!* and *Love Lies Bleeding*; for Belvoir: *This Heaven* and *That Face*; for Bell Shakespeare: *Twelfth Night, The School for Wives*. Lee's most recent directing work outside of Griffin includes *Rupert* for Melbourne Theatre Company in 2013, which toured to Washington as part of the World Stages International Arts Festival in March 2014 and to the Theatre Royal, Sydney in November 2014.

Elizabeth Gadsby

Designer

Elizabeth is a Sydney based production designer. Her set and costume design credits for theatre include, for Adelaide Fringe and Edinburgh Fringe 2015: *Cut*; for Sydney Chamber Opera: *Fly Away Peter* and *An Index of Metals*; for Spectrum Now Festival: *Orfeo ed Erudice*; for Belvoir: *Cinderella*; for Sport for Jove: *Much Ado About Nothing*; for Perth International Arts festival and W.A Ballet: *Epic Fail*; for The Hayloft Project and Rock Surfers Theatre Company: *The Boat People*; for Buzz Dance Theatre and Awesome Festival: *Ecobots* and *Plain Jane*; for the Little Baroque Co (London Handel Festival 2013, Brighton Early Music Festival 2014, and Petworth Festival 2015): *Bach Coffee Cake*; and for the Sydney Conservatorium of Music's Centenary: *The Bernstein Mass*. She is a current recipient of the Australia Council for the Arts 'Art Start' Grant and a City of Sydney 'Creative Living Work Space' Resident.

Luiz Pampolha

Lighting Designer

Luiz Pampolha's credits for Griffin Theatre Company include: *Emerald City*, *The Call*, *The Serpent's Table*, *The Story of the Miracles At Cookie's Table*, *The Nightwatchman*, *The Kid*, and *Concussion*; for Sydney Theatre Company: *Rabbit*, *The Removalists*, *Love Lies Bleeding*, *Saturn's Return*, *Waiki Hip*, *The 7 Stages of Grieving*, and *Romeo & Juliet*; for Belvoir: *Brothers Wreck*, *Antigone*, *Ruben Guthrie*, *Don't Take Your Love To Town*, and *This Heaven*; for Sydney Opera House: *The CODA Collective*, *danceTank* and *Emergence*; for Bell Shakespeare: *Twelfth Night*; for Australian Chamber Orchestra: *Kreutzer vs Kreutzer*; for Sydney Chamber Opera: *The Cunning Little Vixen*; for Pinchgut Opera: *Griselda*, *Castor et Pollux*, *The Chimney Sweep*. Luiz is a graduate of NIDA, and a member of the Illuminating Engineering Society of Australia and New Zealand. He was nominated for best lighting design in 2006 and 2007 at the Sydney Theatre Awards, and for a Green Room Award in 2010. He has also designed productions for international arts festivals in Edinburgh, Wellington, Belfast, Adelaide, Sydney and Melbourne.

Steve Francis

Composer / Sound Designer

Steve's credits for Griffin include: *The Bull the Moon and the Coronet of Stars*, *Between Two Waves*, *This Year's Ashes*, *Speaking in Tongues* and *Strange Attractor*. His other theatre credits include, for Sydney Theatre Company: *The Battle of Waterloo*, *After Dinner*, *Switzerland*, *The Long Way Home*, *Mojo*, *Travelling North*, *Sex with Strangers*, *The Removalists*, *Tusk Tusk*, and *Rabbit*; for Bell Shakespeare: *Hamlet* and *Henry V*; for Melbourne Theatre Company: *The Weir*, *The Sublime*; for Belvoir: *Angels in America*, *Babyteeth*, *Ruben Guthrie*, *Baghdad Wedding*, *Keating!*, *Paul*, *Parramatta Girls*, *Capricornia*, and *Gulpilil*. For dance, Steve has composed music for *Lore*, *Belong*, *True Stories*, *Skin*, *Corroboree*, *Walkabout*, *Bush* and *Boomerang* (Bangarra Dance Theatre) and *Totem* (The Australian Ballet). His recent compositions for the screen include music for feature film *The Turning* and *Stories I Want to Tell You in Person* (ABC TV). His awards include the 2003 and 2012 Helpmann Awards for Best Original Score and one for Best New Australian Work in 2003. He has won Sydney Theatre Awards in 2011 and 2014.

Charlotte Barrett

Stage Manager

Charlotte Barrett's theatre credits as a stage manager include, for Sydney Theatre Company: *Battle of Waterloo*; for Force Majeure: *Jump First Ask Later*, *Nothing to Lose*; for Queensland Theatre Company: *The Effect* (co-production with Sydney Theatre Company), *The Mountaintop*, *Youth Ensemble Showcase 2013*, *Stradbroke Dreamtime* (Remount); for Matthew Management & Neil Gooding Productions: *Thank You For Being A Friend*. Her theatre credits as an Assistant Stage Manager include: for Queensland Theatre Company: *Gasp!* (co-production with Black Swan State Theatre Company), *Macbeth*, *Other Desert Cities*; for Opera Queensland: *The Perfect American*; for shake & stir theatre co: *Animal Farm* (Queensland Regional Tour). Charlotte has a Bachelor of Fine Arts (Technical Production) from QUT.

Kate Box

Sofie Amsel

For Griffin Theatre Company Kate has appeared in: *Tender*. Her other theatre credits include: for Red Line Productions: *Dolores*; for Belvoir: *A Christmas Carol*, *Food* (co-production with Force Majeure)and *The Business*; for Sydney Theatre Company: *Macbeth*, *The Wonderful World of Dissocia*, *Doubt*; for Malthouse: *Knives in Hens*; for STCSA: *Attempts on Her Life*, *Talk to Me Like the Rain and Let Me Listen*, *Hot Fudge*, *Central Park West*; for Bell Shakespeare: *Two Gentlemen of Verona*, *A Midsummer Night's Dream*; for Brink Productions/Windmill Theatre: *The Clockwork Forest*; for Brink Productions: *4:48 Psychosi*s; for B Sharp: *7 Blowjobs*; for Darlinghurst Theatre Company: *Miss Julie* and *I've Got the Shakes*. Her television work includes *Soul Mates*, *Old School*, *Rake*, *Paper Giants: The Birth of Cleo* and *Offspring*. Films include *The Daughter*, *The Little Death* (AACTA Award nomination 'Best Lead Actress in a Feature Film'), *Random 8*, *Oranges and Sunshine*, *The Black Balloon*, *Hush* and *You Cut, I Choose*.

Steve Rodgers
Johann Wertheim

Steve was nominated for best actor at both the Helpmann and Sydney Theatre Awards for his role in Griffin Theatre Company's *Eight Gigabytes of Hardcore Pornography*. For Griffin Steve has also appeared in *Dreams in White*. His other theatre credits include, for Belvoir: *A Christmas Carol*, *The Pillowman*, *Measure for Measure*, *Cloudstreet*; for Sydney Theatre Company: *Three Sisters*, *Riflemind*, *Dance Better At Parties*; for Ensemble Theatre: *A Streetcar Named Desire*, *Diving for Pearls*; for Pork Chop Productions: *Last Cab to Darwin*. Steve has appeared in numerous Australian films such as *I Want to Dance Better at Parties*, *The Men's Group*, and *Bitter and Twisted*. His recent television credits include *The Code*, *Old School*, *Slide*, *Devils Dust*, *The Moodys*, *Paper Giants 2: Magazine Wars*. Steve also writes for the theatre, TV and film, and wrote and co-directed the play *Food*, which Belvoir and Force Majuere toured nationally in 2014. Last year Steve won the inaugural Griffin Lyscraties Prize for *Jesus Wants Me for a Sunbeam*.

Mémé Thorne
Park Chun-hei

Mémé began her career in physical theatre in 1980 with the International Research Theatre Group 'Kiss' in the Netherlands and has worked extensively in Australian Theatre, TV and film. For Griffin Theatre Company Mémé appeared in *Songket*. Her other theatre credits include, for B Sharp: *Empress of China*; for Bondi Pavilion: *King Lear*; for Jigsaw Theatre Company: *Emma's Dynasty*; for Harlos Productions: *King Lear*; for the late Jean-Pierre Voos: *Salome* in Townsville. Her solo works include: *Flossing the Bride*, CPW 5 (Sidetrack) and *Dance Collection 95* (Performance Space); *Burying Mother*, CPW 6 (Sidetrack) and the Sydney Asian Theatre Festival, Belvoir Street, 1996; *Nobody's Daughter*, Sidetrack and the Brisbane Festival (1998); *The Spider Witch*, Tropic Line Theatre Company, for Brisbane Biennial 1999. Mémé was a presenter on *Here's Humphrey* and *The Curiosity Show* in the 70s for

Channel 9 and has had guest roles on *Wildside*, *Murder Call*, *All Saints*, *Love My Way*, *East West 101* and *Home and Away* amongst others. Mémé was cast in two plays for Playwriting Australia's Play Festival 2015 at the Adelaide Festival Centre: *Rice* by Michele Lee and *The Silver Alps* by Maxine Mellor. She has been a member of the Performing Arts Advisory Committee of Asialink Arts for a term of three years and has been a proud member of Actors Equity since 1978.

Kaeng Chan
Chung Dae-hyun
Singapore-born and raised in Australia, Kaeng made his television debut co-hosting the popular preschool program *Playhouse Disney* for three seasons with Monica Trapaga and Colin Buchanan across Australia and Asia. Kaeng's stage credits include Jonathan Biggins's *Australia Day* for Melbourne Theatre Company/Sydney Theatre Company, *Macbeth* for Singapore Repertory Theatre, *Macquarie* for The Alex Buzo Company/ Riverside Theatre, *The Empress of China* as 'Shen Tai' for East Coast Theatre/Belvoir B Sharp. Kaeng has also appeared in musicals, including: *Pinocchio the Musical* for SRT/VizPro, *Jerry Springer the Opera* at Sydney Opera House, *Mame* for The Production Company, *Miss Saigon* for Louise Withers & Associates. Kaeng's TV Credits include *Packed to the Rafters* and *Home and Away*.

ABOUT GRIFFIN THEATRE COMPANY

For nearly 40 years, Griffin has been dedicated to bringing the best Australian stories to the stage.

Griffin produces an annual subscription season of four to five Main Season shows by Australian playwrights, and co-presents a season of new work with leading independent artists. We also support artists through professional development opportunities, including artist residencies and masterclasses.

Griffin is a major force in shaping the future of Australian theatre: it is a home for the courageous and the curious, for the imaginations that inspire us.

GRIFFIN THEATRE COMPANY
13 CRAIGEND ST
KINGS CROSS NSW 2011

02 9332 1052
INFO@GRIFFINTHEATRE.COM.AU
GRIFFINTHEATRE.COM.AU

SBW STABLES THEATRE
10 NIMROD ST
KINGS CROSS NSW 2011

BOOKINGS
GRIFFINTHEATRE.COM.AU
02 9361 3817

Our stage is the historic SBW Stables Theatre, a centre for artistic excellence, discovery and ingenuity.

GTC
RHO
IEM
FAP
FTA
IRN
NEY

STAFF

GRIFFIN DONORS

Income from Griffin activities covers less than 40% of our operating costs – leaving an ever increasing gap for us to fill through government funding sponsorship and the generosity of our individual supporters. Your support helps us bridge the gap and keep ticket prices affordable and our work at its best. To make a donation and a difference, contact Griffin on 9332 1052 or donate online at griffintheatre.com.au

STUDIO PROGRAM

Gil Appleton
James Emmett & Peter Wilson
Limb Family Foundation
Sophie McCarthy
& Antony Green
Rhonda McIver
Leigh O'Neill
Geoff & Wendy Simpson
Danielle Smith

PRODUCTION DONORS

Our 2015 Production Donors supported Angus Cerini's *The Bleeding Tree*, in 2016 help us make Alana Valentine's *Ladies Day*.

Production Partners
Gil Appleton

Production Patrons
Peter Brereton
Robert Dick
Richard McHugh
& Kate Morgan
Richard Weinstein
Tina & Maurice Green
Jon & Katie King
Bruce Meagher &
Greg Waters
John Mitchell
Rachel Procter
Steve Riethoff
Simone Whetton
Carole & David Yuile

SEASON DONORS

Commission $12,500+
Darin Cooper Foundation
Anthony & Suzanne
Maple-Brown

Main Stage Donor
$5,000 - $10,000
The Sky Foundation
Abraham James

Workshop Donor
$1,000-$4,999
Anonymous (5)
Antoinette Albert
Dr Gae Anderson
Jane Bridge
Alex Byrne & Sue Hearn
Richard Cottrell
Ros & Paul Espie
John & Libby Fairfax
Jono Gavin
Peter Graves
Larry & Tina Grumley
Judge Joe Harman
Libby Higgin
Margaret Johnston
Richard &
Elizabeth Longes
Elaine &
Bill McLaughlin
Dr Stephen McNamara
Ian Neuss &
Penny Young
Martin Portus
Sue Procter
Pip Rath &
Wayne Lonergan
Merilyn Sleigh &
Raoul de Ferranti
Diana Simmonds
Mike Thompson
Jane Thorn
Adrian Wiggins &
Siobhan Toohill
Paul & Jennifer Winch

Reading Donor $500-$999
Anonymous (4)
Angela Bowne
Bernard Coles
Fiona Dewar
Max Dingle
Wendy Elder
James Hartwright
Jacqueline Hayes
Michael Hobbs
Susan Hyde

Daniel Knight
John Lam-Po-Tang
Jennifer Ledgar & Bob Lim
Rebecca Macfarling
Lisa Manchur
Carina Martin
John McCallum
Anthony Paull
Alex Oonagh Redmond
Karen Rodgers &
Bill Harris
Catherine Sullivan
Isla Tooth
Judy & Sam Weiss
Simone Whetton

First Draft Donor $200-$499
Anonymous (4)
Jes Andersen
Wendy Ashton
Robyn Ayres
Melissa Ball
Pamela Bennett
Julie Bridge
Jennifer Blair
Rob Brookman & Verity
Laughton
Wendy Buswell
Bryan Cutler
Eric Dole
Susan Donnelly
Tim Duggan
Michele Dulcken
Elizabeth Evatt
Corinne & Bryan Everts
Michael & Kerrie Eyers
Matt Garrett
Sheba Greenberg
Jennifer Hagan
Ross Handsaker
Elizabeth Hanley
Will Harvey &
Ester Harding
John Head
Janet Heffernan
Danielle Hoareau
Mary Holt

C John Keightley
Ross Kelly
Jatesada Kongdum
Carolyn Lowry
Ian & Elizabeth MacDonald
Rob Macfarlan &
Nicole Abadee
Stephen Manning
Christopher McCabe
Patrick McIntyre
Duncan McKay
Nicole McKenna
Kent Carrington McPhee
Dr Wendy Michaels
Keith Miller
Sarah Miller
Neville Mitchell
Kate Mulvany
Kerry O'Kane
Annie Page &
Colin Fletcher
Mario Philippou
Crispin Rice
Rebecca Rocheford Davies
Ellen & Trevor Rodgers
Julie Rosenberg
Catherine Rothery
Dianne & David Russell
Gemma Rygate
Julianne Schultz
Jann Skinner
Augusta Supple
Sue Thomson
Benson Waghorn
William Zappa
Aviva Ziegler

We would also like to thank
Peter O'Connell for his
expertise, guidance and time.

Current as of 28/07/2015

GRIFFIN FUND

The Griffin Fund is a new initiative focusing on education programs, leadership pathways for artists, touring Griffin productions and international exchange opportunities. Donations to the Fund are pledged for a three-year period. It is an investment in the future prospects of the company and the artists we work with. For more information please visit griffintheatre.com.au/support-us or contact our Development Manager on 9332 1052.

GRIFFIN SPONSORS

Griffin would like to thank the following:

Government Supporters

Australian Government | Australia Council for the Arts

NSW GOVERNMENT | Arts NSW

CREATIVE CITY SYDNEY

Patron

2016 Season Sponsor

SBW Foundation

RE:

Production Sponsors

HOLDING REDLICH

nabprivatewealth   nab

Foundations and Trusts

MALCOLM ROBERTSON FOUNDATION

COPYRIGHT AGENCY CULTURAL FUND

ROBERTSON FOUNDATION

GIRGENSOHN FOUNDATION

Company Lawyers

MARQUE

Associate Sponsor

Brett Boardman Photography

Dining Partner

OTTO

Company Sponsors

Time Out Sydney

THE UNIVERSITY OF SYDNEY PERFORMANCE STUDIES

Tatler SYDNEY

bourke street bakery

Rosenfeld, Kant & Co. Business & Financial Solutions

MOPPITY

QUEST Potts Point Serviced Apartments

AVANT Card

CURRENCY PRESS

oxygen

Qbt CONSULTING

SIGNWAVE NEWTOWN

Coopers

FOUR PILLARS

Griffin Theatre Company is assisted by the Australian Government through the Australia Council, its arts funding and advisory body; and the NSW Government through Arts NSW.